FAR FROM THE SHALLOW

Linda Musleh

Far From The Shallow
Copyright © 2020 by Linda Musleh
lindahala@outlook.com

No part of this book may be reproduced or transmitted in any form or by any means, electronic or mechanical, including photocopying, recording, or by any information storage and retrieval system, without permission in writing from the copyright owners.

Cover Design by Kat Savage of Savage Hart Book Services
Edited by Sara Bawany
Formatted by Christina Hart of Savage Hart Book Services

ISBN: 978-1-716-77108-8
ASIN: 978-1-71677-089-0

First Edition

DEDICATION

*From the depths of my heart to
anyone sea deep in feelings,
for anyone on the shallow side,
there must have been a time
you were far from the shallow.*

LETTER TO THE READER

Behind every story, there are mysteries, and behind every mystery, there is another story. I will speak from my heart as truthfully as possible, and you can choose what you want to believe. My words might unfold another side to this story, but I hope you feel the beauty of a heart that thrives in a reservoir of truth. Swim with me far into this sea, and I hope you can feel the love I hold within. I can't promise you won't drown, but if you promise yourself you will learn how to swim, you can save yourself; that's when love will save you too.

You wonder what my story is about? It is about an escape from heartache that nearly broke me. My story is an adventure far into creativity, a search for renewing hope and light, seeking a way out of the dark. The art of ***letting go***, the art of saying ***goodbye***, while dealing with the most painful experiences of life and love. Yet, hoping the end is brighter than I ever thought it would be.

Through my words, I hope you can sense, learn and see that love is about willpower. Love is about equality, sharing humanity to build peace and harmony. Love can be tragic if it's about surviving and not living life. There will always be deep secrets buried within the seven seas, for shorelines are haunted with whispers of tales untold that stay together through the wild and the calm. This is a story of such secrets and lies revealed. "Far From The Shallow" is a story about *pain, trauma, abuse* and *loneliness*. It is a story about *strength, vulnerability* and *healing*, but also a *true survival* tale of hope.

TABLE OF CONTENTS

DEDICATION i
LETTER TO THE READER iii
TABLE OF CONTENTS v
FAR FROM THE SHALLOW 1
INCAPABLE OF LOVE 3
WE NEED TO KNOW WHEN LOVE IS TRUE 4
REFLECTION 9
LOVE'S DISGUISE 11
LILAC NOTES 12
DEAF 13
WARY 14
MOON GUIDE 15
FREEDOM 17
BENEFIT OF THE DOUBT 18
LOST 19
BLACKMAIL 20
NEEDLE AND THREAD 21
TRANQUILITY 22
ROCKY RIVER END 23
PEACE IN THE RAIN 24
FORGOTTEN IN SILENCE 25
NEW ROOTS 27
DELUSION OR AMNESIA 29
LESSONS 30

CHASE THE DEMONS AWAY	31
BLOOMING	32
MY GUARDIAN ANGEL	33
FOUR-LEAF CLOVERS	35
WAKE-UP CRIES	37
LOGIC	38
BUTTERFLY EYES	39
ENDING THE CYCLE	41
FAITH	42
WARNING	43
MY BIRTHDAY	44
SELFLESS	45
BRANCHES	46
WINTER NIGHT	47
LIBERTY	48
FINDING MY VOICE	49
MAGICAL CLOUDS	50
THE SUBCONSCIOUS	51
SURVIVOR	52
COLD	53
TRUTH BE BOLD	54
MATURITY	55
BRAVE	56
LESSONS LEARNED	57
COURAGE	58
LONGING	59
HIDDEN TRUTHS	60

SELF-WORTH	61
THE SPIRIT OF A MOTHER	62
HUMANITY	63
SOUL CONNECTIONS	65
LOVE IS LIGHT	66
PARACHUTE	67
REAL EYES	70
POSSESSION	71
LOST GIRL	72
BURNED OUT	73
IF ONLY	74
RECOLLECTIONS OF UNLEARNING	75
NATURAL LOVE	80
BROKEN TRUST	82
STARLIGHT	83
MISTAKEN	84
UNRAVELLING	86
LOST AND SAD	87
IRREPLACEABLE	88
MY HEART	89
HOW	90
PRICELESS	91
SELF-CARE	92
SAVE YOURSELF	93
GASLIGHTING	94
NARCISSIST	95
THE DEPTHS OF FORGIVING	96

CLARITY	98
ABANDONED	99
AN END	100
CYCLES	101
YOU'RE NOT ALONE	102
CRITICAL CONDITION	103
PUPPETEER	104
WRITE YOUR WAY	105
TRUTH TO HEART	106
DON'T COME BACK	107
RUNNING WILD	108
BE MINDFUL	110
THE WILD AND THE CALM	111
HER LOVE	112
FAR FROM HOME	113
DANCING WITH DOLPHINS	114
RELEASED	115
OPPRESSION	117
AN UNWELCOME STAY	118
SILENCE	119
BOUQUET	120
WEATHER WARNING	121
CHOOSING THE LIGHT	122
ANXIETY	123
LOVE	124
BREAK FREE	125
A HEAVY HEART	126

PROJECTION	127
CLEANSING	128
BREAKTHROUGH	129
A BRIGHTER PATH	130
SELF-ACCEPTANCE	131
HOPE	132
OVER YOU	133
GOODBYES	134
LIMBO	135
FAR FROM HEALING	136
INDIFFERENCE	137
STAND TALL	138
DISMISSAL	139
ANGER	140
THE ODDS	141
BLIND LOVE	142
HOME	143
HEALING	144
WATER	145
THE WHOLE PUZZLE	147
THANK YOU	148
AN ANGEL	149
INNOCENCE	150
PROTECT YOUR SANITY	151
HAPPINESS	152
ONE DAY	153
HOLLOW PIT	154

TRUTH	155
A BRIGHT GIRL	156
EMOTIONAL SUPPORT	157
STRENGTH	158
NOSTALGIA	159
THE IMAGERY OF LOVE	160
DETOX	161
FADED TEARS	162
SWEET RAIN	163
AN OCEAN OF TEARS	164
A RARE SOUL	166
INNER POWER	167
CHOICES	168
YOUR PRESENCE	169
TOO LATE	170
PEACE	171
PATIENCE	172
NEW WOUNDS	173
SNAKE PIT	174
LETTING GO	175
THE BEAUTY WITHIN YOU	176
I UNDERSTAND	177
GROWING PAINS	178
BETTER FOR ME	179
LIFE	180
DREAMS	181
TO BE LOVED	182

SAFETY	183
STRONG	184
GREY DAYS	185
UNLOCKED	186
LOVE LIKE A SEA	187
ACCEPTANCE	188
DREAMER	189
MERMAID	190
SELF DOUBT	191
WEEPING WILLOW	192
MOONFLOWER	193
INSTINCTS	194
EMPATHY	195
A CRAZY PLANET OF PAIN	196
GROWTH	197
OPEN BOOK	198
UNTIL THEN, MY LOVE	199
ALONE	200
BUTTERFLY	201
DEAR GENTLE SOUL	202
A NOTE FROM THE AUTHOR	203
ACKNOWLEDGEMENTS	207
ABOUT THE AUTHOR	209
THANK YOU SO MUCH FOR READING.	211

FAR FROM THE SHALLOW

Every attempt I made to be positive didn't last long. Eventually, I swayed like waves of water into different directions. I wasn't thirsty for love anymore; I was thirsty for life. The sea vines had me twisted, back and forth. The sharks nipped at me for perpetually lingering and the turbulence awoke my inner resilience. There were too many secrets that the fish in the sea knew about me, but no one knew all the secrets between the ocean waves and me.

When I love, I don't quit. I cannot find it in my heart to stop caring. My love doesn't die for those I care about. I've shared an abundance of my life experiences and reached a stage where if you asked me if I'm okay, there would be plenty that I couldn't say. So I've painted colourful pictures of peace to mask the shadows of pain.

I've resisted mourning our disconnection, knowing you were still within reach. And I refused to believe that we were better off apart. Thus, fate insisted on disconnecting us and I have to accept that together is not meant for us. I've written several letters to you after our inevitable breakup that created piercing pains in my heart, evoking grief in my soul. Because my hopes of a happy ending with you was embedded in me. I can't help but pause and ponder on memories reminding me of hurtful, yet critical lessons. I have always deserved to know my value and stand by it. I know I deserved the same commitment, loyalty and respect I gave you to the end. My heart's gullibility worked to your advantage, regardless of your wrongs, despite my screaming intuition. Anytime you said, "I love you," I believed you. Because I felt a connection between my heart and soul to yours. I believed that my undying patience was necessary to give us a fighting chance. I've traveled broadly, hoping you would see the unlimited chances to meet me with some degree of stability, but that was a trick that patience played on love. I bought you time to continue your masquerade and that cost me my life as I was convinced to stay with you.

Every attempt I made to be positive didn't last long. Eventually, I swayed like waves of water into different directions. I wasn't thirsty for love anymore; I was thirsty for life. The sea vines had me twisted, back and forth. The sharks nipped at me for perpetually lingering and the turbulence awoke my inner resilience. There were too many secrets that the fish in the sea knew about me, but no one knew all the secrets between the ocean waves and me.

Linda Musleh

INCAPABLE OF LOVE

I wanted to believe you
when you said you cared about me.
I yearned to feel your arms around me
I mean, I had to ask you for a hug.
I needed your love
and your body language
radiated hostility.

My tears unleashed your anger.
I just asked for love with one hug
you didn't think to give
instead, after hours of
swimming out of tangled grief
I heard you say,
the words, "I love you,"
"what was that?"
"what did you mean?"
I needed you when I was falling apart
I lifted your hands for a hug.
I had to show you how to love.

WE NEED TO KNOW WHEN LOVE IS TRUE

Sometimes the words, "I love you" can be said habitually; it doesn't mean it's true.

Have you ever cried out to someone you love and begged that person to help you keep the relationship on steady ground? If you are successful in saving a relationship that means the world to you, then you're fortunate to know the words "I love you" are true. Because many people are not that fortunate. Many people are experiencing agitation in their relationships and no matter how deep they go, or how high they climb to save them, they can't break the fall.

It's crucial to have the ability to protect your emotional wellbeing and examine any relationship you may be in.

If your loved one has rejected you every time you cried and tried to make the relationship work, don't you wonder what this love means? If, after being blamed for every collapse in the relationship, could hearing the words, "I love you" fix anything? If you intended to stay committed to someone while they were disloyal to you, how could hearing the words, "I love you" feel true? Most importantly, if you take more time apart and communication is still dysfunctional then, is it really love? In this case, it's incredibly heartbreaking and confusing when voicing what matters to you is ignored or wiped away with a storm. Yet, you heard the words, "I love you" so many times. Of course you'll have questions roaming your mind. It's as though saying, "I love you" erases problems in a troubled relationship without effort to resolve issues. It could feel like you've been brainwashed over time to hang on and pretend nothing was wrong. And sometimes, holding on is suffocating and hurts more than letting go, but you don't realize it at the time because you want to fix what's broken.

Holding onto an illusion of a loving relationship hurts more than the reality of it.

Sometimes we learn in agonizing ways that "to love someone" doesn't guarantee you'll be loved back. A loving relationship should feel like you are with a partner that grows in love, not out of love with you. Saying, "I love you" should be accompanied with gestures of compassion and companionship. If you're in a relationship that makes you feel lonely, unheard and misunderstood, then your relationship is in critical condition. You'll know you loved someone if letting go feels like daytimes have turned into nightmares. You'll know your love wasn't returned when you have a dark hollow ache in your chest, with or without that person.

Sometimes broken relationships can leave scars and all that's left to save is yourself.

Because scars run deep, they can be constant reminders of pain and suffering. Heartache can feel crushing when you learn that someone you loved and desperately wanted to be happy with, didn't feel the same in return.

Sometimes people yearn for love to the point that they numb their minds from painful realities. You might have given all that you needed and ended up depleted if you were with the wrong person. You might find your open heart has just a speck of love left for yourself. And that's when learning to love yourself can be a substantial struggle in life.

No one is really happy living a lie and you have your limits. I promise you, you do.

If you have reached your limit, please be gentle with yourself. Please don't regret being vulnerable. You will realize that it's okay to be vulnerable, but with people who respect you. Please don't regret being trusting. If you do, it's okay to feel that way for a while. It will take time to heal and to safely learn how to trust. Please don't be cruel to yourself for forgiving someone who lied to you. Start forgiving yourself and keep forgiving yourself. And please don't be hard on yourself for being soft. Your softness is a jewel, a rare gift to have.

Remember: The wrong people will have distaste toward your strengths and the right people will admire you for it.

You know what true love is. It's rich, like date syrup. True love suffices; it sticks by you no matter the weather. If you ever feel that the words "I love you" are nothing but thin air, you shouldn't ignore or doubt that feeling. It's tragic to feel like love is dying inside your heart, like your soul is lethargic and you have no fight left in you. But you are not alone.

There are plenty of others who have experienced what you have. Reach out because you will find a hand. There are people who care and can help you. We are human beings; we are meant to live life, not to live and feel like death at the same time. We all need to help ourselves, help each other. Guide yourself far from lies and live closest to the truth.

We all need to know when love is true.

Don't forget this: When someone has repeatedly disregarded your efforts of peacemaking, it means they were with you for the wrong reasons and you're better off without them. Because you deserve to feel a love that is true to you.

REFLECTION

When I give my heart to people who haven't earned my trust, my instincts strike back with agony. My intuition declares war on me for disregarding its warnings. My mind recollects countless pieces of evidence for when my feelings were dismissed by those who didn't value me. Some might say they care, but I know a lie when it happens unless I put aside my own worth. And believe me, I've been there. I've tried to engage in self-affirmations and avoid expectations of anything from anyone except self-care and integrity. I've cultivated my soul to a steady pace to deal with messy situations. And how did I find the strength to make limitations between my heart and others'?

I've implemented physical activity to avoid exhausting myself mentally and emotionally. I've tried to stop dissecting my mind and splashing empathy like waves onto shore. Overall, the only path that truly matters is that which leads to self-respect. There has been a bundle of agony in me that wouldn't budge and felt tight on my chest. My wounds have not closed and dried, sometimes they feel strong enough to choke me to death if I'm not careful. I pay attention to the thorns on the flowers that grew with me, because they cut me from time to time. I've knocked on closed doors whilst my heart bled until my skin was smudged with red. My blood has thinned out, and pins and needles have poked at my bones. My soul holds the remnants of yesterday but sometimes, soft ocean breezes sweep them away.

I've gazed at the moon to soothe my tears with no questions asked. And I've made trips to meet the shallow end of the sea, to find a reflection of me, wondering, *"Who could I be?" "What has become of me?"* I still could not see the pain overwhelming me.

LOVE'S DISGUISE

I suppressed my better judgement
to oblige to your satisfaction.
I resisted questioning you
based on my instincts
and despite all my love
I didn't understand why
you often asked me,
"what's wrong?"
despite all my love
you couldn't hide your curiosity
about my coping with your distance.
Despite all my love
you thought I was oblivious
to the darkest secrets in your eyes.
You often asked me,
"what's wrong?"
hoping your secrets were safe
hiding behind my love.

LILAC NOTES

It was the morning after
and my mind blocked out
the night before.

I opened my dresser drawer for underwear.
While my hands brushed by satin so feathery,
an evocative fragrance settled in me
and triggered flashes of sharp glares
from eyes blazed with fury.
I felt a familiar worry,
and numbing of emotions.
I slipped deeper
into a time when fingers
curled around my neck,
they felt like clamps
squeezing my vocal cords.
My mind relied on silence
not in fear of another, incapable of
dealing with my soul's suffocation.
My heart consumed every inhale
I saved shallow breathing for bed,
to stop the reality of feeling dread
to stop the insanity of being blinded,
to stop crying . . . to stop screaming
to stop talking to ears that couldn't hear me.
I gently fell to the floor, baffled by
waves of memories as the scent of
lilac rose from my lingerie drawer.

DEAF

My private escape was under the sea, not a sound could be heard from my cries. I left a dense silence behind because you gave me no other choice. While I loved you blindly, you were deaf to my voice.

Have you ever realized that even though love can blind some of us, it can make others deaf to us when we try to speak up? Silence is sealed and the damage is done because the wrongs are watered down as a means of denial. And while silence may be a way of survival for some of us, it may be a control tactic for others.

WARY

I could not love you
without cheating myself.
Devoting myself to you drained me
into a pit of loneliness.
My devotion to you was pointless.
While learning to be wary of attachments
your withdrawal from me
sank deeper into reality.
I desperately wanted to believe
you shared a bond with me.
I couldn't handle the thought of
you giving up on me.
And gradually, I lost respect for you
because I learned that I was wrong
to think that you could be
as loyal to me as I was to you.
When we split apart
and I tried to save us
I hurt for the both of us.
I crashed many times caring for you
more than I did for me.

MOON GUIDE

I reached a stage in my life where I had no choice but to learn to eliminate the toxins of betrayal and follow the light of love. As countless truths were twisted into veils of distraction, I had to accept the reality of ongoing lies and unanswered questions. I coped with agony due to chronic blame games which blocked me from awareness of persistent and perplexing behaviours. I felt trapped, as though wrapped in a coil of vines. The majority of my life involved fighting for love with patience and silence. My battles lead me to find strong signals pointed in the direction of the moon. The moon wouldn't neglect me and I couldn't neglect it either.

I've walked into tall walls and endless trails, leading to indirect goodbyes. It's no wonder my surpassing efforts to retain pieces of stability between us felt like a crash and burn - I almost perished trying to make a relationship work. And while I loved you on empty, I learned that hate could be real. I didn't feel it to believe it; I observed the rigid face of it, I heard the scalding words of it. And slowly, almost completely, my love for you dulled down. Because I couldn't relinquish myself to you, as you continued to do what you knew hurt me. I stand for what I believe in and I believe that love deserves to be honoured. I believe that love lightens more frequently under the direction of the moon.

FREEDOM

There are those who suffer under the mounting grief of unhealthy relationships. They might become fixated with thoughts of repairing any cracks they see on the sidewalks of their journey, without realizing that the responsibility is not always on them. For those who explore a never-ending path of hope, yet stumble on darkness, they are close to finding light. Those who fall into a downward spiral might hold on to anything for love, even in hopes of renewing it. If you understand the pain of earning this strength, then you understand unmeasurable patience. You need to be free and you might not know if you have the energy to deal with anymore chaos. Yet, you deserve to feel proud of aiming to survive through critical times, especially if you learned to overcome the pain of detaching yourself from those you sacrificed your life for. When you have a heavy ache to bear, it's challenging to remember that you're deserving of self-care. It helps to remember that if your vascular system filters toxins from your bloodstream, then your soul can filter gloom from your heart and mind too. Just know that if you have the patience to overcome your worst experiences, then you have more patience for the best yet to come. Because there's no freedom like the ability to feel, heal and grow.
And you need to be free.

BENEFIT OF THE DOUBT

I believed white lies
because they were prettier
than darkness and never
as ugly as fear.
I doubted my instincts
despite being proven right.
I was willing to continue
forgiving you until,
you tried to turn
my instincts against me.
I was never clueless
as to how far you could
overstep boundaries
I just wish . . .
I wish my doubts
had been wrong.

LOST

As I'm mindful that our time is limited in this world, I cannot help but wonder if one last goodbye or a kind farewell would instill a sense of closure about our past, without worrying that you'll lure me back into a wired web. And I laugh at myself because I know an old joke when I hear one. I've broadened beyond my mind and body. I've stayed with you, wreathed in your smoke to fit your narrative of providing you ease. I understand that time closes in; it's not giving us any more space than it already has. The truth about love needs to be nourished or it will vanish. And that's where I lost myself and felt helpless. I waited for you to turn around, to finally hold my hand on solid ground, to end my struggle for love. But waiting has an end too. I have passed it. I have crossed all roads leading your way and you tossed love away.

I found myself completely lost before I knew, I let go of you.

BLACKMAIL

Your whispers and kisses
misled me into a tunnel vision
because truths were withheld
and promises were made, not to keep
only to silence my voice into a deep sleep.

Linda Musleh

NEEDLE AND THREAD

I knit two stitches
three more and sigh.
I knit four stitches
five more and cry.
I knit six stitches
seven more and ask,
"Why?"
I knit eight stitches
nine more and I try.
I knit what you cannot
ten, eleven more times
a sweater to keep me warm
for when I say,
"Goodbye."

TRANQUILITY

Frozen specks of clouds
sparkling over the sea
giving hope beauty.

Linda Musleh

ROCKY RIVER END

I was a river tide
splashing through rocky valleys
and you opposed my every wave.
I turned into a mist
forming streams of tears.
I twisted and twirled
around all your edges.
You said you wanted peace
though you couldn't make pledges.
My palm prints dried
like soil that was cold
on your musky-scented skin.
Still, when you needed me
my body would unfold
to move the stones between us
my tides, my cries
led us closer to an end.
On odd nights a sharp draft
called to remind me
the unity I thought we had
was not a reality.
And I dashed around an illusion,
crashing into a tragic conclusion.

PEACE IN THE RAIN

There is a girl who believes that thunderstorms call on the heartbroken and paves the way for lost souls. She picks up her slippers instead of slipping them onto her feet because she loves feeling her bare soul hit the ground like lightning. When thunder blares, no one can hear her run out the door. While others curl up in their beds from fear of the storm, she's afraid of never being able to uncurl herself from a broken love. She doesn't forget the feeling of falling over sharp edges that cut her deep. There's a girl who imagines that a heavy cloud of rain could sink to meet her level and whisk her away from the struggles of heartache. Today, her wounds look like jaded flowers and she turns to water as her saving grace. There's a girl who glides through the storm for survival, finding love and peace in the rain.

Linda Musleh

FORGOTTEN IN SILENCE

I don't expect you to remember me
while you soak in your own needs.
Forget me, forget when I brushed
my softness against your bristled beard.
I remember feeling golden,
like a sunset sky broadening your horizon.
Did I fuel your fear of heights,
unleashing my passions onto you?
You craved my skin at night,
waking me from a deep sleep
because your morning gloom
hovered like shadows.
And shades did you well
as you were hung over
by the silhouette of the night before
when your hands marked me.
I gave you my melody
and buried my wounds in lies.
Forget my cries,
use my pain to satisfy your demons.
Forget the last time you looked in my eyes,
forget my scars and use my healing.
Inhale the essence of me.
Forget my heart when I had your back
and you could breathe
without a second layer of skin,
it was easier to master your next win.
I don't think you fall asleep.
I think you trip on sleep

Far From The Shallow

in fear of dreams, in lack of remorse,
and you roll out of bed
like a morning thunderstorm.
It wasn't my footsteps that woke you,
what woke you was my silence
not in compliance with yours.
Because you wanted to forget me
and I'm unforgettable.

NEW ROOTS

On some occasions I've caught your eyes following me. Your gaze brushed by me with remnants of a familiar longing. And I questioned what I was doing in plain sight of you, knowing most of what had changed was my tolerance to pain. The consistency of hurting created dents on both sides of my rib cage. It wasn't as much a matter of letting go and moving on as it was a subject of damage to the heart and soul. Because the last storm between us left me with the sharpest wedge in my being, pushing me over the edge, and into a depth of no return. I don't believe there's a way I could show you the distance I've travelled. I've suffocated in shallow shadows countless times. I've also suffered in the freezing darkness of the ocean floor. And I returned to shore for you. Yet, if you behold the world I've endured when I hoped for forever with you, it would mean heaven has landed on earth.

I've been accustomed to thoughts about our past encounters. I understand what I could barely ever do. I hated saying "no" to you. My heart sinks when I think of walking away from you if you approached me again. If you reach out to me for another rendezvous, I would have to pull myself apart to resist you. Because I need to stick to boundaries. The suffering I've endured doesn't vanish after months on end had gone by without your effort to say one word to me. I cannot forget that you dismissed my past relentlessness to communicate with you. And you have abandoned me in my darkest hours. I cannot habitually take back unchanged ways. Nor will I accept invisible quarter turns when time and time again, I rotated full circles and back for you. I deserve better than to be disregarded and regarded, only at your convenience. I've received your echoes of turbulent motions. And your glances at me confirmed that you picked up the volume of my silence in return to yours. I've sensed your curiosity of my coping alone. It's no secret that I'm no longer in touch with meeting your approval because I learned where that stemmed from. I've ripped out the roots of old weeds and planted daffodil seeds. I wish I could say, I'm glad you haven't made a move. But I cannot shake feeling pity for you, for what you don't apprehend about growth and healing. I wish you knew.

I know you sensed the change in me because I've seen you cower at the sight of me. Your anger is like a winter flurry when you've lost power. And when the fragrance of the daffodils I planted touch your senses, you'll finally see a renewed strength in me.

DELUSION OR AMNESIA

Amnesia settled in on me
wiping away a storm's debris
swirling me periodically
creating fairytale stories of me,
being your dream bride
a perfect compliment to your pride.
I didn't want to believe
in anything other than,
a happily ever after
because it was with you,
with you, I shared real laughter.
Despite your ruffles behind my back
even when I endured panic attacks,
I needed to believe you cared for me.
I thought your sweetened words were true
but that was an illusion that served you too.
How did amnesia settle in on me,
wiping away a storm's debris?
How did amnesia play a part in me or
did I plant delusions, absentmindedly?

LESSONS

If you've settled below zero and you know you can rise from a cold dark place, you can combat fear of the unknown. By the will to learn, you can grow and understand your highest potential. Those who minimize and belittle others forget when they were most in need. So don't forget those who stood by you from the very beginning of your journey. Forgive those who denied you through your worst times for they cleared your blind spots. Learn a lesson from what you thought was a blessing. And you'll realize that a real blessing is the willpower to make room for improvements when you rise from a fall.

Before you take to heart any harsh and constant criticism from others remember, earth is inhabited by unsatisfied souls. Think about the lengths you've taken and the strengths you've mastered to hold your head above high water. Don't forget that the toughest times of your life lured you into becoming a stronger person with sharper vision. No matter what your struggles are, never quit on yourself, keep going, GO! Believe in yourself, release your strengths, and don't settle for less. You are capable of everlasting love and when you find your substance, you will find a brighter world. You will know learning love is what life is deserving of.

CHASE THE DEMONS AWAY

Bad habits are like demons that possess your life. You don't quit bad habits; bad habits quit on you when you learn to focus on exploring your inner truth and implementing a source of fuel to cleanse and revitalize your soul. Challenge yourself to face evil whispers and starve temptation. Make time to figure out what you need to do to take back your life. Commit to a balanced self- care routine. The consistency of total self-care is crucial to eliminating bad habits because everything in you is connected and corresponds. The willingness to make improvements on a broader level means you can do better for others, not just for yourself. And while doing better for yourself, you can do better for a nation. If you open the cage of bad habits, you are creating an exit door for oppression. Healing can be agonizing. Because while learning healthy habits, you are relearning your worth and that will send the demons back to hell without you.

BLOOMING

Pleasing to behold
petals curl, forming shadows
and roses unfold.

MY GUARDIAN ANGEL

In memory of an exquisitely bright soul, I fall back on times when I was young and afraid. I reminisce about an early stage of adolescence, before I was plunged into a life that was planned for me. I was alone in the corner of a room at my grandparents' home, burrowed into sorrow and a recognizable, floral scent floated toward me. My tears were like home and the dark was my blanket; it kept me still and hidden from the hands that dealt with me. "*Not a breath, hush . . . not a weep,*" whispered my mind. I hoped my blanket wouldn't slip away. I had to be sure I wouldn't be seen bending over my bare heart and shrinking soul. Suddenly, the darkness was lifted by a glow. I heard the tender sweep of an angelic body glide down beside me. She rested her wise and graceful hand on my shoulder. And that was the moment when a day of agony diminished far into the past. I could finally breathe light into my soul. I wanted to carry her in my heart and protect her forever. I wanted to save her too. For she served lovingly and prayed genuinely. She guarded more than her own weight and made strides. She kindly understood and patiently listened. The same week she passed away, I had a dream of her face flashing before me like sunshine. My gratitude to her is to secure remembrance of her light, despite the chaotic and messy realities of life. I know her as the greatest woman I have ever spent time with. She was a magical healer. She was beyond a mother and more than a grandmother; I will forever adore her. In memory of a blessing and my mother who made me believe in heaven more than ever before. You are forever in a garden of my heart, **my guardian angel.**

FOUR-LEAF CLOVERS

My adoration for flowers stems from my childhood years in search of four-leaf clovers. Since four-leaf clovers are exceptional and rare to find, I spent much of my summertimes outdoors, exploring parks and gardens. I picked up a habit of plucking dandelion heads, closing my eyes and making a wish before blowing apart the florets. The popular myth that four-leaf clovers bring good luck is no controversy. As I grew out of childhood and could differentiate between myths and facts, I understood a four-leaf clover's mission was to reveal impeccable beauty. Before learning that the four-leaf clover represents a mutation of a white clover and before reading the historical associations related to it, I've always had an instinct that each leaf on a four-leaf clover has a centre bolt of mystical meaning. It can represent different themes depending on your perception. I find the four-leaf clover to be a representation of the four chambers of the human heart. I believe that one leaf symbolizes love, another symbolizes faith, and the two other leaves symbolize hope and truth. The heart has the ability to feel compassion and faith, to lift the spirit with hope, and to accept the truth. Consistent patience, gratitude, compassion and self-reflection are key components to feeling your whole heart's capabilities. And that symbolizes the rarity of four-leaf clovers. The most beautiful blessing in life is to be able to feel all of your heart's parts. Thus, four-leaf clovers are reminders of what we are lucky to have. Love, faith, hope and truth is in you, it's in me, and we can give much more!

Linda Musleh

WAKE-UP CRIES

I often cried
when waking up
from false dreams of you.
I cried more often
when waking up
from true nightmares of you.

LOGIC

I wanted us to stay together
but ocean tides change weather.
I wanted us to stay together
still, clouds grow heavier
I wanted us to stay together
yet, rain doesn't last forever.

Linda Musleh

BUTTERFLY EYES

There may be times when you feel like you are in a labyrinth of despair and darkness has taken over you. The most prevalent mystical aspect of the unknown is the black of the night. Galaxies swallow x-ray lights that explode and renew, appearing and disappearing. It makes sense that the dark is bold and deep. At least once you've closed your eyes and felt yourself slip and fall. We're in a universe encompassed by movement and amongst all creatures breathing in the particulars of the world, therein remains mysteries. Yet, nothing compares to the elegance of a butterfly, its vision is made up of six thousand lenses; imagine the art of liveliness it holds. If you feel consumed in a labyrinth, try to remember that a caterpillar grows in a similar environment before it transitions. When you see a butterfly, it can see you as a star, diminishing any possible darkness because it picks up very high frequencies of light waves. Butterflies have four colour receptor cones and can see ultraviolet lights. So keep in mind that you emit a glow that you cannot discern. For even when you're lost and frightened, you can rise like a butterfly, born by a heart filled with desire. And darkness cannot take over you because you are brighter than you know. Now try, try to imagine your light through a butterfly's eyes and remember if it can get through its most challenging times, you can too.

Linda Musleh

ENDING THE CYCLE

One day I will rotate
in your mind and you will
remember all of me
when you lose me
because by then,
I will have found myself
finished revolving around you.

FAITH

I've traveled through the same cave for most of my life. My feet are blistered, my heart is sound, and my mind has a swarm of wishes. At times, prior to stepping forward, I've paused for moments of meditation and prayed for paradise to brace my soul. I've kept my hands together abiding by hope, creating the figure of a dove soaring toward the sky. I've craved everlasting stamina, in anticipation of driving myself beyond the blank walls of constriction. My self-affirmations have strengthened my dreams of ascending from the underground and meeting a celestial body for safety.

My understanding that failing is part of prevailing, has enabled me to climb steep hills and fall from exhaustion to recall that *"I'm resilient."* The splash of a stream's melody refreshes my creativity and awakens a yearning to dance in a shimmering meadow. More so, I wish for my soul's desire to securely propel me into landing next to a heart that can sing along with mine.

Linda Musleh

WARNING

I heard your footsteps
and turned to the opposite direction.
I sensed a magnitude of gloom
and swiftly walked away
hoping a different scenario
wouldn't catch up to me.
My mind somersaulted in recollection
of times when my prayers were tears
to days when I lay with you in temporary bliss.
Still, your efforts to flatter me
grasped me, almost as intensely
as your countless attempts to flatten me.

Suddenly, I'm slapped with reminders
of a beast exploring passion.
I would be dust if I gave into
every ounce of his fake compassion.

MY BIRTHDAY

My birthday, it's not just a day I was born
it's a day to acknowledge
what brought me here.
All that has happened to me
all that I've experienced,
all that I've loved
and all that I've felt.
Every day is closer to the end
and still a beginning.
Hiding hurt is no talent of mine
because I can breathe in tears
but I cannot keep them back.
My mind wants to travel
yet, my heart is stuck,
sticky like molasses
staying sweet, sweeter.
I cannot call love a lie
love is a reality of life
cutting death shorter,
training my heart to let go
when it was built to hold on,
teaching my mind to say, "goodbye"
when it was built to stand by.
Oh, the days ahead
may be surprises to share.
I can dream and prepare,
work and execute.
My birthday, it's not just a day I was born
it's a day to make my wishes come true.

SELFLESS

Since my life was arranged
and times have changed,
my heart expanded
while my healing stalled.
Life didn't feel real
and during quiet, late nights
adapting alone, I wondered,
"How did life speed by?"
as I nursed my child and wept
growing more affection,
for the little ones that slept.
I gave them my heart
filled with stars, forever.

BRANCHES

A psychologist once told me, "You are barking up the wrong tree" and we both didn't realize how strongly the tree held its branches over me.

I've met psychologists of extraordinary knowledge and ability. However, medical professionals couldn't help me unless I welcomed a different approach to my healing. I needed to deal with myself and my lack of validation. I opened my eyes to the flip side of my mind in order to comprehend a psychologist's point of view. I listened to the knowledge that professionals shared until I was ready to apply their advice to my life. Seeing myself through the expecting eyes of those in my family tree, gave them a hold over me. And seeing myself through the eyes of those who were humble towards me, freed me from captivity under the wrong tree.

Linda Musleh

WINTER NIGHT

A cold breeze
flooded my lonely space
leaving me with a lace of
shivers tracing my bones.
There was an aura of fear
swallowed by fury
a creature's favourite ability
to deny vulnerability
a dark, dense cloud rolls
looming over fearless souls.
A fallen icicle trickles
down soft skin,
winter is inevitable
and unforgotten.

LIBERTY

For my survival
I climbed out of old rubble
and took back my rights.

FINDING MY VOICE

I've tolerated the confinement of oppression and underestimated the power of depression, consuming me into a deeper silence. I've had a long chain of sorrow wrapped around my heart. I couldn't break free from a cell I called love. How could the word 'love' be applied to feeling handcuffed and heartbroken, trying to use my voice? The chain I'm referring to grips me like one wound attached to another and another, holding my soul hostage. I learned to stretch out the stress from my body. And without a loyal hand I grew fonder of earth's ground. I learned to rewrite the definition of love on sand. I learned to expose my wounds to the sun for a kiss. And I sang in the sea where I was most embraced. For what I thought was love was really a lesson, leading me to healing. And writing freed me too. I had to splash my voice onto paper, water, or any open channels because I couldn't ever swallow my voice again.

MAGICAL CLOUDS

My heart tensed with pain
I gazed at clouds expanding
and hope fell like rain.

Linda Musleh

THE SUBCONSCIOUS

I wished falling asleep
was the safest way
to avoid thinking about you
yet, my subconscious
hit me like a sledgehammer
crushing any piece of
unconsciousness I could find.
The reality between us
burned away my loving dreams.
Even if I could absorb a sense of
solace in a peaceful sleep
the reality between us
whipped me with a ball of
fire across my face,
stinging my brain
and waking me up with pain.
I'll never forget my lessons learned
remembering the crashes and burns.

SURVIVOR

After heartbreak
every step you take
is like walking a high wire
you need to be meticulous
moving forward without a fall,
because you're already carrying
a wounded heart and soul.

COLD

Sometimes I wondered
about your soul
if you were present at all,
when we lay parallel to each other
in a pitch-black bedroom
and my tears fell
as you turned your back
the distance between us grew
and the less we were together
the more deafening
and chilling the silence.
You were so close, yet so far,
and the further away
from me your heart beat
I wondered how you survived
without any body heat.

TRUTH BE BOLD

My silence was never stronger
than when I walked away,
because my words were just a blur
to those who lied everyday.

MATURITY

I would be naive to believe that knocking on the door of denial would be welcomed like I would be, unwary, trying to break down a stone wall when I was already battered.

Some people give others the silent treatment because they choose to deny their vulnerability and that gives them a sense of control. Whereas, some people cannot accept barriers of communication and need to express themselves. Through experience and study of healthy and unhealthy relationships, you can learn the difference between the denial of human feelings for a need to control, and the protection of human feelings for the need to survive.

BRAVE

I understand ill habits
I know they can be deadly.
I don't think either one of us
was ever, really ready,
to admit it wasn't love
making our hearts unsteady.
There were odd, rugged aches
residing in my tailbone
numbing my feelings,
feeling alone
and I couldn't tolerate
another crippling cycle
that would lead me to my grave.
Thus, I put an end to our storms
because one of us had to be brave.

LESSONS LEARNED

I wish I cared for my heart
before I gave you my all.
I wish I knew my strengths
before you stifled my soul.
I wish I caught myself
before our first nightfall
because I was the only one
who could save my body, after all.

COURAGE

I faced all my fears
fighting a feeling of gloom
and I rose in pain.

Linda Musleh

LONGING

The scent of a rose
and a river valley flows
in search of desire.

HIDDEN TRUTHS

You dream while asleep
what's concealed when awake:
your innermost truths.

SELF-WORTH

When people value standards like they value their loved ones, their actions speak volumes about their truths. Mutual understanding and responsibilities are communicated and shared as contributions towards maintaining a healthy relationship. When the responsibility of keeping a relationship intact is shifted only onto one person, that person will most likely become depleted and hurt. If you uphold your principles and listen to your inner voice, you'll learn the skill of discernment too. Once you learn and practice self-worth, you will know who cares about you and who doesn't. If those who matter to you are within reach, make time to check in on them. Because any kindness you give adds beauty to your self-worth too. **Securing self-worth is crucial.** Be cautious to balance the respect you give between yourself and others. Don't wait for better changes to come your way when you can go there yourself. Don't dwell on regrets when you can learn from mistakes and focus on what's best for you. Most of all, be sure you're true. Truth is as clear as the ocean blue and it has an inevitable power to reflect your value.

THE SPIRIT OF A MOTHER

A mama bird is ready to take flight for her fledglings when in need, and so will I, stretching my arms out like wings.

Being a mother has hauled me out of the darkest pitfalls and triggered a passion in me, to believe in the treasures and entity of the sea. I saved myself when I learned that I deserve to be cherished the same way I adore my children. I saved myself when I forgave myself as much as I could forgive others too. I have made mistakes and mistakes have happened to me. I have been near death, but death is in the back seat of all I had to defeat. There's a power in me that has survived drowning. My heart is a reservoir of my love and my children are the milestones of my heart's strengths. My life will not downgrade because one person couldn't love me back, nor will I fade away if hundreds of people despise me. What's a spirit without a heart to flourish in? And my spirit bloomed, bearing beautiful children. I've run through fires and walked on wires. I've been swept by high tides and been left barely holding onto mountainsides. Yet, I sprang from the deluge of darkness. And I stayed on standby in case my children needed my shoulder for a cry. A mama bird is ready to take flight for her fledglings when in need, and so will I, stretching my arms out like wings.

HUMANITY

Some people enjoy helping others. They can listen and understand your expressions and concerns. Sometimes all you need to do is reach within your heart and unlock your voice. You might not realize that it's okay to ask for help until you've tried. It's okay if things don't work right the first time. It's not easy to speak to someone who can listen without any judgements. We've all judged and criticized ourselves, in turn, we could unconsciously do the same to others. There's no being perfect with one another, but we need to be human with each other.

If you know someone can understand you, then speaking to that person will allow you to hear yourself and process what you've internalized. Sometimes all you need is to feel heard and less trapped. True friendship takes time and is not always going to happen the way you want it to. Maybe you can listen to others and give wise words of feedback, yet, when you're dealing with yourself, you cannot follow your own advice.

Maybe you valued someone and a relationship with that person more than you valued yourself. But remember, you are sufficient for yourself without anyone else's approval. If you've been rejected or hurt by others, it doesn't mean anyone else you cross paths with will hurt you too. Don't allow oppressors to succeed in shutting out the voices that need to be heard. Your heart broadens when you love yourself as wholeheartedly as you love your dear ones. You're a beautiful creation, deserving to be understood and worthy of love. When you step into parts of the earth that welcome you, you will learn that there's more humanity in the world than you think. There are people who need you and can appreciate your heart. Keep your humanity strong and help love grow in a world that needs it now, more than ever.

SOUL CONNECTIONS

There are soul survivors: people who join each other spiritually. There are soul survivors with the same mindsets or different ones; still their hearts associate, somehow and in some way. We may feel challenging depths of pain that seep through our veins and manifest into works of art. There are always routes open for understanding and learning. When you think you're alone, remember, there are spirits you cannot see, taking time to keep you company. The moon listens as the oceans sing, bringing people together and pulling them apart in mysterious ways.

You will find yourself and connect with the person that will love you for all of who you are.

LOVE IS LIGHT

Perhaps when you think you might be blinded by love you are really misguided by the company you keep and you're missing out on the light of the moon.

Maybe it's not love that's blinding you. Perhaps your light has been blocked by indifference and you need to pay heed to your company. Let your heart guide you into a nourishing environment like the moon shines comfort on lonesome souls at night.

Linda Musleh

PARACHUTE

I've had bad days when I felt my spirit sinking and my heart pounding through my chest, as though I was on a hot air balloon that unexpectedly deflated. And days like those trigger overwhelming emotions in me.

Through immense pain, I learned the importance of boundaries in relationships and it made sense to set limits with my emotions too. Emotions are temporary, but most of the time they are connected to experiences and relationships with others. I discovered that detaching myself from the grips of an unhealthy relationship was extremely complex and ignited flames within my being. I learned to release the toxicity of hurting as it was far more beneficial than keeping it lodged in my throat. And I accept that sometimes my tears will fall like my heart would drop if I were skydiving. I use my lessons from past experiences to deal with distress like a skydiver would use a parachute for safe landing. When I immediately face my intense feelings, I'm putting a halt to an accelerating fall and saving myself from a harsh breakdown. I couldn't set boundaries in my relationships unless I felt crushed. So I suffered, juggling with learning to set boundaries whilst calming my inner clashes. I've had bad days that provoked self loathing thoughts and triggered a need to numb my feelings. I realized that pain is necessary to gain insight on my struggles and cope with them.

Difficulties can turn into inflated balloons when emotions rise, which then leads to a heavy fall.

If I cannot balance my emotions, then I'm magnifying and prolonging the reality of my stressors. I learned that the depth of heartbreak will depend on what I hold on to and what I let go of. I questioned myself, "how much of myself was I burning for love?" But the better question is, "do I want love to consume me?" "Do I know when I need to set a limit to hurt?" "Can I find a safe platform to set my trapped cries free?" I can swim or sail the sky to let go of my heart's pain and relieve any chaos in my brain. It's rewarding to practice the ability to distinguish between rational and irrational thoughts. Because I need to make sense out of my mental stress and do my best to take care of it. Truths have stabbed me in my heart but at least that eliminated lies. I have ignored my instincts, but they come back to haunt me because I have a strong conscious for reality. Without accepting reality, how could I, how can I be my own saviour?

If you have ever had the feeling that something wrong was going to happen before it happened, then you should know that trusting your instincts is an invaluable skill. Because in some situations, doing the right thing might result in unfavourable outcomes that can be intimidating. And sometimes relying on your own experience and intuition is all you can trust. Understanding the reasoning behind my emotions and the actions I take will determine if an experience is a lesson or a blessing. The sooner I use a reasonable mind to control my feelings, the easier it will be to steer away from the strong winds of a bad day. Balance is the guide to thrive, not just survive. And if I happen to be on a hot air balloon that deflates at an unexpected time, my survival skills will be my parachute.

REAL EYES

There are eyes that if you looked into
you would see a soul giving, relentlessly,
absolutely frantic to make changes
a heart that could bring
a whole new life to love
and a whole new love to life.

There are eyes that if you fell into
you would sense an energy
as intriguing as the sea waves
under a full moon.

There are eyes that if you read into
you would acquire the bravery to swim
far from the comfort of the shore
to risk your life out of love.

There are eyes that if you smiled into
you would appreciate the ocean
and the sky reflecting blue
out of real love for you.

Linda Musleh

POSSESSION

I couldn't feel
your soul next to mine
despite your arm being around me
when we were lying in bed
I wondered,
was it for the sensation of
having my body next to yours
for the sake of formality,
for the purpose of tenancy?
and my voice was locked,
my mind was numb
my thoughts were blocked
because I didn't know,
if it was safe to speak or move,
so I stayed in the still moment of
our bodies touching
because it was ultimately,
better than nothing.

LOST GIRL

I lived life searching
for the girl I used to be
she was lost in me.

BURNED OUT

Desperation plus delusion
equals a lethal combination of
hearts in a black hole,
resulting in hope burning out
and turning into stardust.

IF ONLY

I wish you held
the weight of my mind,
holding on to you.
I wish you felt
my stumbles into chaos
to spare you stress too.
If only you chose
to be acquainted
with my merciful soul.
I wish you felt
the despair in my hand
when I gave you control.
If only you knew loyalty
is a must to gain trust.
I wish you tasted my tears
on the darkest of nights.
If only your heart and mind
could hear my lonely fights.
I wish you could lean closer
to the sun and grow with me.
If only you could feel
the kind of love
that lasts an eternity.

Linda Musleh

RECOLLECTIONS OF UNLEARNING

I know that I deserved to be treated better. It was easy for you to call me crazy. But what's really crazy is your idea that my body was tailored to suit your needs. My soul withered while I abandoned it, submitting to your hungry demands. I let you harbour my body and you left me to deal with my soul's cries in an empty bed. Your regular nothings slid by me because the rare little things were like miracles. I don't know how I mustered the strength to adjust to your prolonged withdrawals. It was excruciating to detach myself from you because whenever our bodies engaged, I was deep in feelings and you were in the shallow. After a life of witnessing your anti-sympathetic manners, I knew that if I ever caught a glimpse of repentance from your eyes I would never forget it, but I have no recollection of remorse from you. I would have to be a robot not to feel worthless, being unseen by you. Even when we had broken chords and shattered glass between us, I felt compassion for you, not pity and I was sad that you couldn't see my heart melting for you. No matter what I did, no matter what I do, I cannot change what you are unwilling to understand.

I speculated more often than not, if you were really human, or if it was true when you said that "no one wants me"? You were convincing me that I'm too much for anyone to bear. Yet, you shut down endless chances to express your true feelings in a calm manner. And those endless chances were weapons of convenience in keeping me submissive. Well, I'm human. I exist. I matter too. Just like the sun feeds light to the living, love should illuminate the heart and soul. Just like a drop of rain makes way to a dandelion needing to bloom. Or the way a cool breeze can lift a spirit on a murky day. My spirit needs to thrive. I know I didn't ask for too much because I let go of many standards to focus on necessities. I know it wasn't difficult to say, "Hello" and break the silence. Instead I was left with memories of unanswered questions, such as when I asked you, "Why the silent treatment?" and you responded, "I don't know," which really meant "I don't want to tell you." What I thought was a marriage, turned into a dark game of hide and seek. We slept between the same walls. I leaned on mending broken bridges between us while you stayed and left every day, ghosting me. I remember the ruthless pain, coping with feeling devalued when you ignored my cries. We knew days, weeks, months went by and nothing, nothing became of us but growing distance. My bones deteriorated for the sake of togetherness. All that remained for me was a recovery plan, or our splitting apart. I had to find broken pieces of myself to unlearn sinking into a bottomless pit.

When I recall my unconditional affection in response to your need for pleasure, I feel nausea that's haunting. I wish you wanted to fight for us as perpetually as I did. I remember when any sense of hopelessness felt like strings from my heart were dangling out of me. I didn't know if you looked for my pain or any attachment at all. I needed to hide when I felt my heartstrings tightening around my neck. I couldn't allow myself to choke from your presence ever again. How could I stand straight within a few feet from you, knowing I didn't deserve to feel shame?

I think of ways I could replace yearning for love to be brighter. And my mind plays the splashing of ocean waves, caressing my skin. I hear songbirds singing. I taste the sweetness of the sun with hints of salt. I travel back in time to visit the water fountains down an old neighbourhood street. I climbed over a green hill to an Italian coffee shop, where I spent many summer mornings writing poetry about you.

My mind recalls the subtle aroma of earth mixed with cocoa lingering through the pappus-filled air. You knew I loved you. We could've learned love together. I thought that's what you needed, but couldn't tell me so, until I overheard you say that my softness and sensitivity was not your taste. Tragically, I had to swallow bitter betrayal. After all the years of trying to change me when I wasn't the problem, you missed out on a priceless growth of gold. The truth is, I deeply loved you. I enabled your needs into a hierarchy and you bestowed upon yourself a throne. Yet, the agony of growing through breakdowns unleashed wounded parts of me that were tamed for far too long. Overall, I had enough strength to accept the truth that you denied. And I take responsibility for the times I adjusted to your denial and my own. I confess to enabling the lies we lived. Because I enjoyed pretending we had the perfect love story for a temporary escape from a deep, cruel reality. Consequently, while I worked on rebuilding my fractured parts, I learned that I exhausted myself fighting for love. And love should never be this draining.

On rare occasions, I felt more terribly lonely and unwanted without you. No matter how betrayed I felt, I wanted you back. I convinced myself that one day we would align in tune like spring tides. Even though I knew my chances of being loved back were next to nothing, I still cared about my dreams. It felt like forever to come to terms with your part in my stormy past. Time was running out to fix the damage done to me. I had to accept that I would spend the rest of my life healing.

Yet, I find myself feeling less envy and more empathy toward those that find true love because the world needs more peace. True love cannot survive in illness and cages. True love is meant to help each other grow and it's a blessing meant to set hearts free for joy.

NATURAL LOVE

I don't believe in anything greater than the process of nature, like the birth of a cherry blossom. I think flowers feel pain when absorbing water, leaning toward sunlight, growing and breathing. Flowers emanate tenderness to us even under strain which is why I believe aches and heart-flutters can be blessings. I have felt dry to a point when I couldn't crave water or sunlight. I only longed to sleep by the moon rays before the sunrise covered my bed. I've slept on thorns and bathed in tears. I've moved so slowly, almost still, not intent on taking from mother earth. I just hoped the sea would give me security. I waited, two days, three days, until the petals of my soul fell, pink, faded into white. And my body collapsed. My soul sensed an awakening of rain pour pending near. My spirit didn't leave my body. I heard a voice that seemed like it was as far underground as the roots of daisies. Whispers of *"Never let go, don't give up,"* roamed my mind. Clouds released the rain. An immense need to recover was never more welcomed. As I lifted myself, dusk approached, and a rose glistened the way eyes light up in love. A beautiful presence bloomed. I moved forward, slightly shrinking at the power of a cold draft. I felt empathy for a yellow tulip that had its last drink. I paused in adoration of nature's elegance, a subtle art, not ready for fading, still giving gracefully. Even the dark makes space for hope that doesn't starve you until you no longer need. And without down-to-earth love, growth is meaningless. Living beings in tune with nature reflect truth. **I don't believe in anything greater than the process of natural love.**

BROKEN TRUST

My forgiveness toward you
was unconditional
I had your back,
although you hurt mine
staying with you
was a promise
sealed with tears
and I swam out of the depths
of anguish for better times
my soul surrendered
in hopes of peace with you
until I learned the secrets
you wanted me to keep were lies.

**There's no trust
and no secrets if there are lies.**

Linda Musleh

STARLIGHT

I've looked at the night sky
in hopes to catch
a glimpse of the moon
if I don't see the moon
I check for one star
and if I don't spot a star
I think about you
wondering,
if you ever felt sad
for two people
who were perfect
for each other
yet, couldn't be together
and I hope you realized that
every time we went for a stroll
and I lowered my gaze
to the ground
it didn't imply that
the wrongs were on me
because we exist
with one sun for all
and while you stayed on earth
I sailed to Venus,
hot and bright
to bring you light,
day and night
if that does not spark hope
then how do stars exist?

MISTAKEN

Honestly, every break I grew up to see had me wishing I could fix them and I didn't know that instead, it was breaking me. My need to protect the ones I relied on drained me because I couldn't stop destiny. I cared until I was skin and bones and of course that was mistaken for anorexia. I was disappearing into a world that gnawed at me and turned me upside down. If there was anything I starved from, it was emotional deprivation, an unheeded cry, pouring my heart into hands that squeezed me dry.

You were barely put in a position to have to explain to me why you hurt me. My forgiveness was your free zone to blame me for your negligence. On the rare occasions that you slipped on covering your own tracks, I listened to you excuse yourself. I knew the truth and denied it to myself because I wanted to hear you say something for yourself. Now, there's no need for explanations to draw more drops of love out of me. I reached my ends when every bit of what I valued, you devalued. Any progress I made toward self-respect had to be re-evaluated based on interacting with you. Now, I can correctly point out what I suffered from and that's a definite step towards healing.

Emotional support is a critical part of a loving relationship.

UNRAVELLING

Life hurls bundles of
lessons into storms.
It's only after
the chaos fades
that blessings unravel
like blooming roses,
moving on appears
to be a mess
when it's nothing less
and only more,
a clean-up
brought to shore.

Linda Musleh

LOST AND SAD

I don't know the tension of
a heart shrinking for a handful of power.
but I know the comfort of
a heart growing for a handful of peace.
I don't think you've ever been lost unless
you didn't follow directions on the road.
I don't think you understand the grief of
giving your heart up in despair
and never having it returned for repair.
When you need your heart the most
you will not be able to find it
if you've buried it with time.

I didn't want to, but I needed to
pull my heart away from you
because I was lost without love.
And no matter the outcome with you
regardless of your version of the story,
I will always feel sad about me and you.

IRREPLACEABLE

If a mirror shatters
it can be replaced
but nothing replaces
a shattered heart
nothing hurts
a fragile heart
like staying broken.

Linda Musleh

MY HEART

I know I should cease
caring so much about you
but I need my heart.

HOW

How do you live
blocking sunlight,
how do you breathe
while shrinking?

PRICELESS

I've lent my sound mind to disturbed ones
my empathy has exhausted my heart
with all the humanity left in me
self-affirmation recharged me and I say,
"It's okay to ask for my peace back."
"It's necessary to keep my sanity."
"It's not bad to say 'no'
"I need to stay out of a black hole."
"No more refills for empty souls."

My sanity is priceless.

SELF-CARE

Use time to heal you
focus on saving yourself
don't care for monsters.

SAVE YOURSELF

If you have a heart that could care for a monster, ask yourself, what that could do to you? If you worry about what the monster can do to you, you're wasting time that could save you. When you think about what you can do for you, you are empowering yourself. You know you need to get away from danger, but you don't want to leave the creature alone. Why would you feel guilty for needing to survive? Don't you know the world doesn't have enough caring souls like you? You are a gift to the world and a monster doesn't change its nature. You deserve to feel safe. You deserve to live a survivor and tell your story. Protect yourself before believing anyone else can. When all those you thought loved you, failed you, help yourself more than you ever thought possible. Self-care is not selfish. It's more than alright to finally save yourself for you.

GASLIGHTING

A deep part of my brain has been
intimate with melancholy
planted memories, invited oppression
and if I questioned anyone, it was myself
which was a breeding ground for you
to turn me against myself too.
I adjusted to meet your hungry ego
see, I understood you
more than the pain of my broken soul,
more than you know
and the irony is: the wrong I tried to fix
was made alright for you instead
my broken bones, I needed to heal
excused you from healing your own
concealing when you mocked me,
using time to coat your words with venom
without using your hands
to break another bone on my body.

Linda Musleh

NARCISSIST

My forgiveness could build you
the steps of a high rise,
but you had no interest
in anything I could build
it was my shrinking
to the bare minimum of being,
to feed your tower of pride
and that is frightening
to step down from
for anyone who fears heights.

THE DEPTHS OF FORGIVING

If you cannot recognize forgiveness, you cannot exhibit it. You cannot learn forgiveness if you're incapable of working for peace. You cannot feel love without opening your heart the same way you cannot taste the sweetness of honey without taste buds. Accepting love is understanding there's a soul under the skin you touch and that's most important to feel. Mercy accepts delicate and vulnerable qualities of being. Love never trashes a treasure to conceal a true identity.

Sometimes, I didn't think there was a matter of forgiving you because I didn't blame you for my hurting. It was never a matter of forgiveness because you had it all and no mercy on my soul. It was a matter of figuring out why you did unforgivable things that many people wouldn't tolerate and would have removed themselves from. Instead, I stayed engaged in the danger zone, exposed and vulnerable because I was intending to make all the wrongs, right. My heart tolerated a mass of grief heavier than our weight combined. When your presence felt fulfilling to me, you flushed me out. You knew I had already suffered an ordeal and thought tossing your hurts on me wouldn't be much harder to bear. You knew I was committed to resolving problems and dashed away to preserve your ego. I was crushed by an avalanche of blame, numb

CYCLES

Wilted flowers melt on graveyards of the dead while bouquets bloom at chapels, ringing wedding bells. Emotions entertain thoughts and hearts bleed. Precipitation of tears relieves drought, causing celebration for good deeds. And joy breaks into sorrow knowing, death is closer than tomorrow. As flowers dress up all occasions, petals begin to peel. Naked stems wither away, marking an end to a life, ending what was real and beginning another turn of a heavy wheel .

Once I was handed flowers to end a stormy cycle, then the flowers died and the truth was bare again. And a new cycle began, then another. I love flowers, but I prefer not to have them to dress up anything, good or bad. Flowers deserve to stay where they are planted, where soil, light and water is the home they need without being ripped apart.

YOU'RE NOT ALONE

Face the palms of your hands
kiss loneliness goodbye
and rest your hands on your heart.
Do you feel the divine company?
the sky is your roof,
your open mind
and the ground is your garden.
Earth cradles you
and the ocean sings you to sleep.
When loneliness whispers,
"you're unlovable,"
"nobody wants you,"
your heart's rhythm intensifies
to mellow your mind
silently saying,
"you are love,"
"you are one of a kind . . ."
because constellations exist as proof
that the universe expands above,
making beauty out of love.

CRITICAL CONDITION

My spirit is weak
for giving my dreams to you
and draining my essence.
My body aches
from bearing your anger
that ripped me apart.
My intuition cries
for ignoring lies
and tolerating disloyalty.
My mind glitches, knowing
while I tried to heal for us
you were buying time to be free.
My heart stresses
for needing to feel yours
because I remember bleeding.
My hope dies a little more
each time you come back to me
and I give you my all
only to realize that
you couldn't love me any less.

PUPPETEER

Like a puppeteer
you pulled my strings and left me
to untie the knots.

WRITE YOUR WAY

For those who are hesitant about sharing their writing: If you feel like you're healing and worried about new wounds, you're not alone. You're at an occupied stop before you move along. Nothing hurts like a wounded soul, especially that of an empath's. Open up to your emotions and treat them with hospitality, like you would treat guests at a party. Create something memorable of them. Write it down, dance it out, sketch it on paper, smudge it with paint, find a beat that moves your soul. Be your own best friend and respect your emotions like you would respect your loved ones'. Draw your way, make your way, fight and light your way, find your way closer to a path full of positivity. Because you need to be grounded while you heal. You can spread light and share your growth as you write your way.

TRUTH TO HEART

I'm honouring my heart
by admitting the truth
I would be lying
if I said I'm fearless
because denying
my fears
messes with my head
and without fear
I would be dead.

DON'T COME BACK

My heart misses the love I gave you. When I remember trying one last time to fix us, I hear the cries of my soul, my tears feel like fire. You were fuel to the pain I could never forget, so don't come back to me.

Going back, if you understood the hope I held on to and the reality I let go of to repair our brokenness, maybe you could see me through the same light that I saw you. Going back, if you could see my heart's clarity, instead of what you thought I should be, you would accept the love and strength in me. Going back, if you could find it in you to feel love for me, you wouldn't have abandoned me when I needed you to fight for us the most. Your coming back to me doesn't mean you can have me, make me whole and break me again. I will remember what I learned as I grew. I will remember and never forget. I'm for keeps, not for leaving and coming back to. You left me for the last time, so don't come back to me.

RUNNING WILD

My healing was not appealing. My skin was peeling. I was bleeding. Each tear I shed created poetry instead. I filled pages with screams and you were still as deaf as silence could be. I found myself wandering in a tunnel, pondering to no ends, screening out sound and adapting underground. My heart flowed like the sea, hitting borders and collapsing on black. I would daze into submission for days. Sometimes my flow of thoughts were broken and rearranged to adapt to the demands of burying my pain. I heard my spirit dying under a rising silence. You pretended not to hear me and now I say, "I was never yours," "I'm not yours." I cried and heard denials until I was moulded into a carrier of pain. My veins hurt like stones were moving with my blood and I broke into a river, running wild.

A few scars rose to the surface of my skin and suppressed memories saved us both from more commotion. All you could say about the scars and the memories was, "It happened a long time ago," "It's gone, it's all in the past." You didn't deny giving me a black eye. You didn't taste the blood that I did when I choked on the thorns lodged in my throat. Instead you called it a curse to be dealt with, to cover your doings behind splitting us apart, and I believed you. Because you thought you had control over all. Whatever the curse, it was only made worse. It wasn't your eyes that my tears burned, it was mine.

I was not yours. You were never mine. I guess my love was too strong for your heart to open up to. Yet, you wanted me and you got me. I had no choice; my heart was chosen, my heart is full of love and I gave it to you. I've been through enough with you to know that you didn't want a prize you didn't have to gamble for. One disaster after another, I thought, "If I lived a lie to my last breath, how could I make the best out of what I have left?" I stood on my own two feet. I didn't need to beg or please. I was alone, yet free, finally pleading with myself to let you go. I was never yours because you were never mine. My blood carried pain, and I cried a river out of blame. You stayed a stone and I, a river, running wild.

BE MINDFUL

We all have the right to understand our own pain and that can be complex. For those who cannot understand their pain, they may not be able to understand the pain of others too. Your life is your journey. You will cross paths with others and there will be an exchange of good and bad. The good and bad doesn't have to be black or white. We cannot live in peace amongst each other without seeing the colours in between. Always remember there's another side, with unknown circumstances behind what is presented to you. Be cautious about making assumptions because answers take much longer to find in comparison to all the questions you may have. You wouldn't be human if you didn't cause pain to anyone your entire life because your entrance into this world was painful. So why not spread empathy? Be the change that enriches and saves lives. Understand yourself well. Being thoughtful of yourself and others means you are being mindful too.

Linda Musleh

THE WILD AND THE CALM

She has a mind of her own
with an untouchable lock of
values and beliefs,
a heart treasure that listens,
but is not persuaded to leave
she believes in her survival
and gives care that's worthwhile
her footprint scars are her guide
to moving ahead,
closer to the day she wishes for,
a day when she can fiercely dance
with her heart in the clouds
and she can rest her soul
like sea tides subsiding to a calm.
There are always deep secrets
between the seven seas.
Shorelines are haunted with whispers
of tales untold that stay together
through the wild and the calm.

HER LOVE

She knows she has herself to lean on
she knows the sun does not rely on
the moon to keep it glowing.
Grass turns to the sun to keep it growing
but she is not grass, nor is she a flower.
She has a heart that fuels its own power
she likes the thunder and the rain
because it drums away her pain.
She stands stronger after cloudy days
she is radiant after storms have made ways.
She fights demons that lurk and breathe lies.
She rises to love like ocean tides.

Linda Musleh

FAR FROM HOME

Home was not the house I went to
it was the love I gave you,
painting red flags into white
the only place I went to
in your arms no matter the fight,
the only place I grew
and learned my lessons
by staying with you
a place I kept drowning in
holding onto you.
I was far, far away from home.

When I needed you the most,
you were only willing
to stand at the shallow end
and watch me drown in the deep.

DANCING WITH DOLPHINS

Diving under the surface of water so deep
I gracefully rise in cottony sweeps
my soul unfolds in curves of satin skin
stretching from limb to limb
aiming, reaching outwardly, rhythmically
spreading my arms and legs free,
through openly blissful motions
arching my back, flexing,
twirling upside down, embracing
senses unwrapping elegance
brushing by bodies
all spiritually encompassing,
blue waves swirl the tips of my toes
to the ends of each strand of hair
into a heavenly abyss of escape
my lips touch a greeting with care
and we dance along enticing spirits
connecting deeper than this ocean
all hearing, sensing, loyal creatures of
the aqua glass window world
beholding mystical treasures for eternity
capturing refractions of elegant melodies,
dancing delicately with dolphins underseas.

Linda Musleh

RELEASED

She cried her last words to him
and whispered, "let me go"
Promises were broken
before they were spoken
plans were carried out
and secrets were kept
alone in the dark, she wept.
Doors of a holding cell shook
walls closed in
she fell deep within
a dungeon,
numbing fears
her skin dripped tears
splattering trust into being
for those who were unfeeling.
Vulnerability had her on her knees
she didn't want the keys
to set herself free.
She just needed to know
if he could really let her go.
Her youth passed by
as though she was in slumber
when she awoke
she was told,
"lost time is just a number."
She learned that
"good girls" were loved
and "bad girls" were resented
so whatever made her wrong

Far From The Shallow

she worked hard to prevent it.
Finding love within her heart
feeling deeply from the start
she questioned submissiveness,
in spite of those who cursed her
she resisted leaning towards death.
She survived to see the sky blue
without always doing
what she was told to do.
It took years of tears to reveal realities,
to face the knots of betrayal
she wanted to be free
from a black hole, this jail.
But she didn't want the keys
to set herself free.
Vulnerability had her on her knees.
She bled and pleaded
her voice was depleted,
she cried her last words to him
and whispered, "let me go."

OPPRESSION

A submissive person is prey to an oppressor. Sometimes people oppress themselves too. Yet, no matter what the reason may be, being both submissive and oppressed is a very painful and complex experience to deal with alone. It keeps you entrapped and in despair. Letting go means you don't need to depend on anyone to validate your love. Letting go means you are responsible for releasing yourself to healing and wellbeing. You don't need to worry or wait on anyone to acknowledge your pain and suffering. And most of all, you don't have to tolerate your grief to make life easier for anyone. This is a devastating experience for those who have experienced abuse because they tend to be selfless. They have been giving the love they need. For this reason many people who are abused take a long time, if not a lifetime, to break free from the control and effects that abusive behaviours have on them, because they don't feel like they are the only ones holding on. Healing starts when oppression ends. You can empower yourself. You can find your strengths, practice them, use them consistently, find yourself and heal.

AN UNWELCOME STAY

My pain is not fierce anymore.
My heart is yearning
for a bath in the sea
my eyes are focused on
beauty instead of debris.
After yelling under waves
my throat is sore
after a day of downpour,
my sorrow is not sharp anymore.
The sun has burned
my nightmares into ashes,
scattered onto shore.
My mind is weary with grief.
My soul craves
a sweet breath of sunset hues,
fate beholds, lessons to be told.
And my healing reminds me
day after day,
my sorrow is unwelcome to stay.

SILENCE

Before I began to blurt out every word of my love and devotion, I didn't stop to think of the times that my honesty backfired on me. When my youthful heart was gullible, I jumped into strong waves activating all the strength in my body, to express my heart as openly as the sea. I've recollected events of yesterday, overanalyzing them in hopes of answers for today. And during the times I spoke to you, I wondered what I missed, unaware that you were angry since the last time we kissed. It's no wonder that my words were not heard. I understood silence as clearly as could be, but telepathic communication never worked for me.

BOUQUET

For every wish
you breathe
write a note.
For every goal
you achieve
plant a flower.
Water your own
special bouquet
and watch it grow
every day.

One day at a time,
remind yourself of
what you've accomplished
and what you can achieve.
Don't give up.

Linda Musleh

WEATHER WARNING

I was captured by your charm
until your rage shook me with alarm.
I tasted ashes and sensed fear of harm
many storms have headed my way
only a few waves swept me away.
I didn't snap out of your trance by chance
day after day, I fought to be free.
I learned that I always had the power in me.

CHOOSING THE LIGHT

It's a speck of light
awakening me
from the darkest shades
revealing masquerades.

It's a spark of positivity
burning out negativity
that cheers my heart
with or without you.

ANXIETY

I've felt reluctant
to share my heartaches
because I've been made redundant
and my story weighs on my chest.
My heart collapses when I breathe
stitched up hollowness breaks open
and a fluttering buzz overwhelms me.
I'm fighting a harsh reality.
I'm tired of toxic memories.
All that makes sense is my tears
giving my soul necessary ease.

LOVE

All the answers
to the questions
about love
are in your heart.

Your mind
is a shield
to your heart.
It takes tears
and time
to put them
together.

Linda Musleh

BREAK FREE

You can break
a narrow path
into branches with
better directions.

A HEAVY HEART

It has always been challenging to keep my head held high while my heart was drowning, holding on to you.

There are many different types of strengths, like the kind that can weigh you down, like too much of a good thing is not really good for you. The strength I'm referring to is that of hope and the beauty of it. Sometimes too much hope or too little of it can be detrimental to your mental health. And it can be tragic when hope is taken away. When hope is damaged, it takes a different kind of strength, like traveling thousands of miles across an ocean, to heal. It takes impeccable strength to renew or build up hope and use the lessons learned to be more cautious and prepared for the unexpected. Because it can be exhausting, struggling to keep your head held high while holding a heavy heart.

PROJECTION

From the start
I gave you
my vulnerable heart
and you learned
exactly how to take me apart.
Is that why you withdrew
did you think I was like you
that I would break your heart too?

CLEANSING

Tears are rain for the heart
making room for growth
nourishing love to stay
and washing the demons away.

BREAKTHROUGH

Fine, call me crazy
for I loved an imposter
and I kissed a monster.
What kind of disasters
have you lost your mind to
and did you shine through?

**I've had to break through
immense pain to feel sane.**

A BRIGHTER PATH

Finally, I found my way out of a maze, amazed to find myself on the outside, looking in through the dark. I found what was taken from me. I gathered my identity without looking back and I gained clarity.

I was expected to fit into the narrative of a traditional role before I was born. When I refused to follow the leader, I was left not only in a jungle, but in a maze as well. I had to unlearn being dependent and didn't know that my right to my identity was stolen from me. I didn't know I was trying to survive a life that was much like the wilderness, until I found myself in another dimension, looking in on the dark. I finally found myself in a community that accepted me. And what had felt like a dead end was just the wrong end. There's always room to change direction because learning is an endless experience much like exploring the wild. Looking back only stalled my healing and kept me lost. Moving forward helped me find myself. Don't allow those who hurt you a chance to dismiss your need to heal. No matter what, stay on the brightest and safest path possible. Keep shadows at bay because they will always be lurking and don't doubt any new clarity that shines your way.

SELF-ACCEPTANCE

When you accept your imperfections
you're not desperate for love.
When you're not desperate for love
you know when you're really loved.

HOPE

Hope can fuel the soul
and enlighten the heart.
Stars don't expect
anything back from us,
they just keep shining
ablaze in the night sky.
Don't let love die.

Hope is not an expectation
it's like stars in the night sky
not allowing light to die,
offering a beginning
to allow for forgiving
reaching out and above
radiating nothing but love.

Linda Musleh

OVER YOU

Surviving a life with you
was like being shipped overseas
and left abandoned
trying to satisfy and fend off
sharks that were fuming at me
and wondering how long
they would stay in slumber
before returning to bite me.
My fears froze my tears
and imagining myself without you
felt like my heartache multiplied.
Flashes of memories burned my mind,
blurring my thoughts.
I was your emotional hostage
or perhaps, just a tool in storage
I was alone, figuring out how
to prevent another tornado
while I was buried under a steep hill
far from recovery, just empty, still
and getting over you meant
never being under you again.
That's why you left me in the deep.

GOODBYES

While I learned to say goodbye to drowning shadows you made yourself a ghost too, not haunting me with lies just with my memories of goodbyes.

Saying goodbye doesn't mean you've forgotten all the love you've felt. The love you had will always be a part of you. Letting go is hard work. Sometimes there's too much emotional investment in loving someone and there are memories that you may need to say goodbye to, otherwise they will haunt you. Saying goodbye is one of the most soul-tearing experiences of life. What's worse than saying goodbye is denying the process of it. Loving someone can be flawed and messy, but to continue loving should become a beautiful experience, not a rotten one. Loving someone should not feel like heartbreak after heartbreak and one goodbye after another. Sometimes you need to have a sit-down with love. You may need to figure out what direction to take based on what you have experienced and what your vision is moving forward. Because saying goodbye can pierce your heart, but loving someone who doesn't love you in return will eat at your soul.

LIMBO

I confessed my love to you
and you left me in limbo.
If I knew my worth, long ago
if I knew what I needed to
I would have left you
without one more goodbye or hello.
I would have left you
with my tear-stained pillow.

FAR FROM HEALING

When I thought you were by my side
I felt as strong as lightning.
When I thought I was safe in your arms
I felt heaven was more inviting.
When I learned that
you weren't really by my side
I lost all that built me strength.
Anywhere I found assurance
I found pieces of me instead
now, I need to find closure
on my own, alone.
Now, I need to heal my heart
on my own, alone
now tell me, how should that be
I pray for an answer
because healing seems to be
as far away as another galaxy.

INDIFFERENCE

We thought we would grow old together
yet, distance grew between us.
If only the thought of growing together
was a commitment to you like it was to me.
If only love opened your heart to me
like it opened my heart to you.

STAND TALL

Every time I rose into light
out of the darkest pits,
my wounds resurfaced.
I felt swallowed by grief.
I couldn't stand tall
without feeling my weakened soul.
I couldn't stand tall
until I fiercely believed in healing
and relieving my heart's pain.

DISMISSAL

Unless you needed me for something I was ~~nothing~~ disregarded ~~without~~ by you.

Sadly, there are people who will consider you of value **only** if they can use you for personal gain. And whenever they do not need you, they will devalue and disregard you. Don't ever allow someone's words and actions to make you believe you're nothing without them. If anything, you are more without them and you don't owe them your value. Maybe it was easy to feel dependent on someone who groomed you with persuasion. Don't blame yourself for trusting appealing promises when you have a kind heart. Don't let anyone make you feel like you're an extension of them; if anything, being treated like a utensil instead of being treated like a human is destructive to your wellbeing. If someone mistreats you this way, the reality is that you have a value they cannot possess. You are a fully capable, valuable, loving soul, deserving of happiness and love too. Don't give up on love. Be independent and be free.

ANGER

I've seen the anger that you hold
it taints love and makes life cold.
I became a ghost of your charade
called crazy and left to fade.
I know alone, thanks to you
I failed myself in loving you.

THE ODDS

It takes two to make 'us' last
where were you?
I confess to fearing
an end between us.
Many late nights,
attempting to repair hope
caused me nightmares.
I still hoped and it felt
like I cried for an eternity.
I tried to beat the odds
and despite the odds
winning against us
I didn't let your demons kill me.

BLIND LOVE

I'll be a stronger me and they will have no clue how I removed the layers of blindfolds and let my new, soft self be.

Regardless of all the betrayal and neglect, I blindly opened my heart and confided in the same people who tore me apart. I blindly tried to make peace with those who couldn't understand me. I blindly gave what I needed, not caring if it was returned. And every time I made mistakes, I awoke soaked in saltwater from the lessons I learned. Then, there were those that made payback a mission and carried it out so well. Yet again, I blindly fell into trap after trap, making it easier for them to treat me like crap. I unknowingly helped some people gradually destroy me. Now I owe it to myself to let them go and be free. I owe myself intensive healing and when I'm through, I will be a stronger me. They will have no clue how I removed the layers of blindfolds and let my new, soft self be.

HOME

Home is not just a house with a price and your name on it. Home is where your heart is, what you carry in it and how you care about it. Do you build hope in your heart? Do you know how to care for relationships using good communication? Is there trust, respect and companionship in your home? There's nothing wrong with calling home a body that carries a heart and soul. There's nothing wrong with calling home somebody who values humanity, sensitivity and thoughtfulness over power, money and fame. Home is where you truly hold gratitude and value love. If you cannot lift a finger to help someone, then at least don't lift a finger to point at anyone. Home is a helping hand, a soft place to land. Home is where you can feel free, supported and safe. Take care of your body, it's your home and your soul will thank you later.

HEALING

My heart's pain is like an ocean
sometimes slapping me
with tidal waves taking me under
while I fight to get to the surface
struggling to breathe.
Then there's the calm
that I never want to leave
I embrace the waves' caress
while I'm cradled
into dreams of nothing less
than how beautiful life can be.
My heart's pain is like an ocean
and that's where my healing should be.

WATER

My soul has been a battlefield for my mind and heart. Attachment to others has torn me apart. My love has been wounded caught in the crossfire. But I found the sea to cool me, hold me close and carry me away, graceful wave by wave healing me tenderly.

I reflect day by day, experience after experience, one thought carried to another and another. I learn more about myself as I heal from my wounds. Water is not just what I love, and swimming is not just my favourite activity. It's deeper than that. I have been submerged by all types of heartaches and felt lost in many ways for most of my life. I have loved deeply, regardless of the toxins in my life. I can feel love in my heart because I learned the difference between an illusion and reality. I have fought for understanding my whole life. If I didn't know any better than I do right now, my mind would still be spinning and I would still be vulnerable to abuse. Swimming is an escape for me, a channel to feel free. It gives me comfort, acceptance and inner peace. Whilst I'm submerged in water, my inner peace does not cease. I don't need wings, for my lungs are like gills. I can float in the ocean or the deepest end of a pool for as long as I please, knowing that water will not drown me the way sadness has, knowing that water does not have closed walls, edges and corners like the ones I have hit face-first. Yet, I have ventured into the deepest parts of the sea and I'm not quitting on my fight for equality. I can grow stronger because I have a unique and most beautiful life-sustaining ally - water.

Linda Musleh

THE WHOLE PUZZLE

He said that I'm a puzzle
and I said,
"of course I am
you took the parts of me
that you wanted and left the rest,
the best parts of me,
unwanted, unheard
and misunderstood."

You can't love in pieces.
Love is whole.
What about the laughter,
courage and calm moments?
What about empathy,
trust and honesty?
What about being
open and vulnerable?
What about the sacrifices,
forgiveness and chances to advance
at communicating peacefully?
Love is not love if it's in pieces.
It's about accepting a person
as a whole, caring,
taking the time to listen
and understand each other
completely and mutually.

THANK YOU

I learned to love myself
loving you
I learned to forgive myself
forgiving you.
I learned to stand up for myself
standing up to you
I learned to care for myself
caring for you.
I learned as agonizing and painful
as my struggles were
in loving you,
I have to say *thank you*.

AN ANGEL

You heard my cries in the depths of despair
as I escaped from a storm wrecked pier
you took my hand and my pout disappeared
then, we walked through a rain garden.
My heart bled as I realized
that you could see the pain feeding on me
yet, you embraced me relieving my inner scars,
shining light to a starless night.
I envisioned the anguish I revealed to you
and felt a shame sinking in on me
but by the end of the day,
your shine grew vibrantly
it revealed that beauty is real as can be
and the ghost of my past was no longer me.

INNOCENCE

A child with a heart of gold
who cares for others
putting herself on hold.
Don't mistake her open heart
as a band-aid for your wounds.
She's stronger than you think
much stronger than she thinks.

PROTECT YOUR SANITY

Confusion plays a part in anguish
when thinking,
"I know what I need to do,"
yet, when the time comes
my heart cannot follow through
failing myself again
"and for what, for who?"

No one is worth risking your sanity for.

HAPPINESS

Like wings are to birds, happiness is to the heart.

Like another new season gradually approaching, I felt my heart again, rising with happiness even though some days were darker and lonelier than nights. I let my open mind be free, allowing positivity to dismantle negativity, for it was worthwhile to know I could still smile. Like wings are to birds, happiness is to the heart, to feel free and leave pain in the past because nothing is promised to last. There is no guarantee of return and like leaves dry and fall, tears rise and drop from grieving eyes to say goodbye to temporary lies.

Linda Musleh

ONE DAY

One day will arrive
when there is nothing left
to bring us back to each other.
One day will arrive
when there are no more
backward steps to take into
making familiar mistakes,
and moving forward with love
will fill the hollow heartaches.

HOLLOW PIT

I was a perfect fit
to fall into
the hollow pit
carved into my heart
because you knew
I liked to swim
in the deep end
and you always chose
the shallow end.

TRUTH

If we could be
truthful with ourselves
like having 20/10 vision
reflection would be sunlight
warming a cold hand,
honesty would be
widespread like a prairie
and we would be spared
from the knots of
emotional pain.

A BRIGHT GIRL

She was the kind of girl
who walked to the park
holding a fiction book.

She was quiet and alone
with a mind of her own,
the type of girl who
didn't follow or lead
she had a heart filled
with stars and dreams.

EMOTIONAL SUPPORT

I've held my tears back, again and again until I was alone because I couldn't trust your intentions and my heart needed my attention.

It's almost impossible to trust anyone who used your deepest sufferings against you. Trust is about honesty. If you've been attacked for being an honest person, then how can you learn to feel safe being honest? How can there be a loving, healthy relationship without trust? Maybe love and lust was confused. But you can learn the difference between lust and love when you realize that physical attraction without spiritual connection does not last long. And when a crucial component such as emotional support is missing in a relationship than love is missing too. If you find yourself holding back your tears and unable to express your feelings in fear of retaliation, find someone you can trust. Even a diary can be your best friend. Once you are able to get the help you need and you know that there are people who can understand your struggles, you will feel like a rainbow is rising in your soul. So cry if you need to, but remember you can learn to trust again when you learn to trust the right people and you will, because you can pay attention to your heart and to your soul's intentions.

STRENGTH

From struggles to strengths
all around she never found
a strength quite like love.

NOSTALGIA

Meditating and stretching reminds me of soothing childhood memories like playing piano keys that touched the beats of my heart. Sometimes, I thought raindrops were falling in the palms of my hands, but they were my own tears, keeping me warm.

I cannot bring back the days that summer breezes felt like gentle hugs and sun rays felt like kisses on my forehead. But I can build the feeling of safety and purity back into me.

Sometimes, a strong feeling of nostalgia took over me, and I closed my eyes, pointing my chest and hands up to the sky. When currents lifted my hair away from my face, I caught glimpses of violets dancing and stardust in the air. In the stillness of the moments, floral, maternal scents filled my lungs. I treasured a bond with heaven and earth, while mellow piano notes echoed all around me. And a natural humming within me awakens when I visit a world of gardens.

THE IMAGERY OF LOVE

The imagery of love
is in abundance
different for you and me.
The imagery of love
can be like a dark tunnel for you
for others, love can be the sun.
Love can be what you want it to be
holding you tight or setting you free,
that's what saves hearts
or that's what breaks hearts.
Because the imagery of love
could be like swimming in the sea,
running away from it all
or standing at shore
holding hands with me.

Linda Musleh

DETOX

Light delivers
rich clarity
when you bathe
in the sun
and decide to cut
the strings of
addiction
one by one.

FADED TEARS

Raindrops fall on me
as a breeze plays with the trees
my tears have faded.

SWEET RAIN

Petrichor is sweet
because rain shouldn't leave gloom
and life needs to bloom.

AN OCEAN OF TEARS

When I could finally breathe all the weight out of my heart, I drowned in tears.

I was subdued for a lengthy period of time in my life. Yet, I had compacted emotions trapped inside me. There were times when anxiety cramped my muscles, and grasped my voice. There were quiet, solitary nights when my thoughts dragged me down a pitch black abyss and caused me to dread my future.

I was healing, but at the same time I was treading water, learning to keep safety in mind because I experienced trauma. I needed to recognize why I reacted out of fear and was easily triggered, even during minor conflicts. I couldn't heal without understanding that I needed a safer environment to do so. When I focused on finding a safe place to breathe and combat my pain, the unresolved feelings of my past flooded my soul. I chose not to run away from the battle between my heartaches and love. Fear, emotional blackmail and any other guilt-tripping experiences that held me hostage to anyone, will never have power over me again. When I could finally breathe all the weight out of my heart, I drowned in tears. I felt cleansed of all the toxins that deprived me of peace. My heart and soul are free to feel all that has been buried within me and self-compassion will help me heal.

A RARE SOUL

My darling,
you are more
than a treasure,
a rare kind of soul
misunderstood
yet, always bathed
in warm colours
and no matter what
when you fall,
you shimmer
because you wear
your heart
like an emerald,
always holding
peace, transparently.

INNER POWER

If she wasn't standing in her own way, no one else could.

She holds an innate ability to love others more than she could love herself, for she enjoys being selfless. Heartbreak is unbearable for her because her hope is never-ending. She honours equality, demonstrating it with generosity. Those who push her away are lucky to still find her willing to forgive and love. As emotional as she can be, she blossoms, learning more about herself than she ever thought possible. She learned to be her own saviour, not belonging and owing anything to anyone but herself. She focused on inner power, blocking attempts from anyone who tried to control her. After all, she learned self-care and dreamed that one day she could reach the sky, because **if she wasn't standing in her own way, no one else could.** No one could stop her from reaching her dreams.

CHOICES

Wherever time goes
it takes and gives
health and wealth
life and love,
so choose wisely.

Linda Musleh

YOUR PRESENCE

When I hug you
I press my ear
against your chest
to hear and remember
the sound of your heartbeat
cheering for your presence
and so will I.

TOO LATE

His promises were like dead flowers they could not be watered because he pretended not to know the lengthy amount of times he chose to be a no-show.

His promises were like one step forward and four steps back. He had tremendous amounts of opportunities to make things right, but instead he withdrew, broke promises and gave up without a fight. When you water a plant that's about to die, it's too late to save it. It's inevitable. Valuables are valuable, only if they are valued.

PEACE

I gathered
all the peace
I made
with my past
into a different me,
until my past
was barely able
to recognize me.

I don't like to think
of getting older as aging,
I like to think of it
as learning and changing.

PATIENCE

She thought she would
never find real love
and that her life was over.
But one day, love found her
and renewed life in her soul.
She was exhausted
because her heart hurt,
giving all the love she wanted.
She stopped trying
when she learned
to save her energy for those who
respected her in return.
Love is not forced
it happens unexpectedly,
and effortlessly, especially
for those who stretch
their hearts open,
needing to replace
emptiness with hope
instead of feeling broken.

Be patient; love finds a heart as big as yours.

Linda Musleh

NEW WOUNDS

I have no choice
except to finally
say goodbye to
an uninvited
visitor from
an old injury
because I have
new wounds,
sinking through me.

SNAKE PIT

It's not wise
to look for answers
or goodbyes
from people
who poisoned you
in every way
with their lies.

Stop digging in
to the same site
where snakes awake
to bite you.

LETTING GO

I used to think letting go meant giving up or quitting. But letting go is not calling quits for most people who feel deeply and passionately about someone or something. It took me a very lengthy and extremely painful time to learn that letting go will happen when it's meant to happen. For me, it felt like a last resort.

Letting go was a path I never believed I would meet and after bearing the disbelief of it, I learned that letting go took me higher than ever.

I've broken so many promises to myself to end destructive patterns. I've been vulnerable, forgiving, trusting and honest to many people, most of whom broke my trust. My heart could be so sad and soft, but not bitter. No matter what, I couldn't give up on faith or love because I knew I felt it. I was left with no choice but to let go of the staggering weight of unrequited love.

THE BEAUTY WITHIN YOU

While you're in the process of detachment, you might pause to look at him and feel what drew you to him. But give yourself a thought too. What about you and the beauty of love within you? Is he seeing you? Is he capable of feeling deeply too? You know the answers if you know you need to let go. And I know you wish it was different. I know you wish there was another firm grasp reciprocating the love you were holding on to. It hurts, but he doesn't need to know about what he doesn't value. If he cared for your love the way you did, then you wouldn't have drifted apart. If he loved you like you loved him, you wouldn't be struggling with heartache. And it would be easier for you to love him and love yourself too. Instead, you're on your own, feeling broken about adjusting to letting go and shivering at the thought of moving on. You have a heart that can love deeply and that's a beautiful power that will enrich your soul more than you know. It's stored within for when you need it the most. Just stay strong. Don't let anything or anyone else defeat the beauty in you.

Linda Musleh

I UNDERSTAND

I understand why
you take pills at night
to help you sleep
because I was like a full moon,
sharing my all with you
and you were holding secrets
like the sky holds stars,
there were too many
not to see some on you.

GROWING PAINS

I grew through pain
and the best parts
were bending in the sun
and bathing in the rain.

**Let growth be your barrier
that protects you from toxicity.**

BETTER FOR ME

I wish I was better for me
than I was for you.

I wish I knew this
when I needed it the most.

LIFE

It just gets harder
to fight clean in a world
that fights so dirty.

DREAMS

Love holds endless dreams
a trace of heaven on earth
a glimpse of heart beams.

TO BE LOVED

Being alone
is like being
your own leader
affirming your love
is how you deserve
to be loved.

I wish for a love
the way I loved.

SAFETY

It's a brave move
to face the unknown,
to take a step on your own,
to realize and learn
what you thought was safe
was actually your danger.

I thought I was safe with you
until you pulled me in
and locked the door.
I thought I was safe with you
until you knocked me out.
I thought I was safe with you
until I learned that
my idea of safe was dangerous.

Freedom is mine too.

STRONG

The best thoughts
can defeat the worst.
The things and people
you thought
you couldn't live without,
proved you wrong
because when those
things were gone
when those people
were gone
you moved on,
you move on
and that makes you strong,
that makes you strong.

Linda Musleh

GREY DAYS

There have been grey days
when anger stirred within me
because my loyalty was slapped
with a mass of deceit.
Yet, steam cleared my skin
to withstand poison.

There have been grey days
when a dear soul listened to me,
it rained after my tears poured
and my heart sang a mystery.

There have been grey days
like collapsing mountains of grief,
throwing a challenge to me
to breathe hopefully
like a well-wisher,
wishing for grey days
for grey days to be richer.

UNLOCKED

Your heart has an unlocked window. It's not so hard to open if you try. Between the sky and the ground, rivers and oceans flow in unison. Your heart has a wide window and if you open it, you might find a vivid, beautiful world outside. You might hear a river tide, flowing softly and subtly. You might feel drawn into it, but be careful not to tame it, or the current will intensify. And if you make it to the river, embrace it, for it fades away when you're not in tune with the unison. Listen to the melody, simple and serene. The motion of the tides enlightens an open heart. Do you hear, or do you listen? Pay attention to other creatures connecting, playfully splashing around you, calming their inner storms too. Open the window to your heart. Let love be seen like a stream that's ever enchanting and never daunting. If you search, you will find a river always, somewhere playing the music of life and easing a lover's despair, always somewhere.

Linda Musleh

LOVE LIKE A SEA

I find peace in the rain
it reminds me of
the ocean, always open
for the way I love,
I love like the sea
and the spaces
between two shoulders
cannot always hold me.

ACCEPTANCE

The sea embraced me
bearing my tears and shadows
promising freedom.

DREAMER

I was never lonely because I had dreams to keep me busy and a sky full of endless possibilities.

A relentlessly hopeful and faithful soul keeps praying, keeps dreaming and doesn't give up on faith and hope. If you believe your prayers are heard then believe your prayers can be answered.

MERMAID

She warms the ocean
more than a scarlet sunset
before the night falls.

SELF DOUBT

I wonder if there's an unknown dark side in me. Maybe I don't know what to believe about myself in fear of demons ruining my recovery. I feel that a journey to self-love will break up blinders within my mind and that's okay. Because every day can be a new way to heal. I have realized that I enjoy discovering more about the world than I do about myself. On some days, I worried that I subconsciously validated my weaknesses to outnumber my strengths. And self doubt was one of my consequences, hindering my personal growth. I'm afraid that the journey to self-love will lead me into the same tunnel of tears, I have tasted in the past. I'm afraid self-love will unfold the truth about those who couldn't love me back. Because I wasn't taught that I deserve love that lasts.

WEEPING WILLOW

She illuminates an enchanted dream
with radiant fireflies and eyes that gleam.
Silken lilac and turquoise wings
spread like clouds of dust
into mountain waves after dusk.
She dreams a dream lovingly
with lightning fireflies and satin-soft skin
she bears the strength of intuition
and reflects the power of tranquility
as steady as a weeping willow tree.

MOONFLOWER

She has a glow
and a thirst to grow
a delicate bloom
during a full moon
mesmerizing at first sight,
reaching out and into the night.
Beware of an essence so strong
her fragrance lingers on.

INSTINCTS

I have the instincts
to spot a play for power
like bees sense nectar from a flower.

Linda Musleh

EMPATHY

Empathy is as painful as it can be sweet.
If I could cut empathy out of me
I would have less tears and much less love.
Empathy is feeling everything,
feeling love and joy
or loneliness and sadness . . .
without empathy my heart
would be a frozen flower.
Empathy pulled you to me and me to you.
The lack of empathy from you
is what drew you away from me,
leaving me longing to touch you
missing the sound of your voice,
connecting one flower stem to another
and one tear falling next to the other,
leaving my skin with shivers
from hints of your cologne
to missing promises wrapped with hugs.
My empathy reminds me of
longing for starlight reflections,
hoping it could touch you too
that's all that I could do.
Because when my love broke apart
I stayed planted in the field where we laid,
catching and holding the flower petals that fell
from the stems you ripped out of my heart.

A CRAZY PLANET OF PAIN

Hurt is my war on depression
hurt is sickening, hovering shadows.
Hurt is fire to my bloodstream
hurt is a shipwreck of bloody screams.
Hurt is splitting my mind apart
hurt is a blade, piercing my heart.
Hurt is a lesson to avoid being vain
hurt is a crazy planet of pain.

Linda Musleh

GROWTH

Every drop of pain to the last
dripped from her past
and she still rose
by will-ignited power,
she grew thorns like a flower.

OPEN BOOK

I was like an open book
I didn't worry about what you took
I just added more pages.

UNTIL THEN, MY LOVE

I dreamed about the love
we could have had.
Until my soul met yours in a dream,
nestled by a pillow of white
and comfort on my heart
sealing security to my instincts.
Then, I was awakened by sunrise
for a new beginning to **my love**
You were the dark I couldn't leave.

ALONE

I was less alone
with thoughts of you, than I was
when I was with you.

BUTTERFLY

I hope you know your strengths
growing out of your pain
and leaving behind a shell.
I hope you know your worth
when you finally rest atop
a branch of smooth-spun skin
that holds you within.
I hope you know your beauty
when you transition to a safer stay,
patiently waiting for your wings
to dry before you fly away.

DEAR GENTLE SOUL

Gentle soul, if you fell
for a liar and a fake
forgive yourself.

Be kind to your nature
because you were real
and true more than ever,
your heart is gold
delicate as a feather
and easy to hold.

Don't blame yourself
for not knowing
a liar and a fake
because you're incapable
of being that kind of person.
You are a lovable human
with a gentle soul.

Linda Musleh

A NOTE FROM THE AUTHOR

Thank you for reaching the last few pages of my book. I have a secret to reveal that will wrap up my story before you put it down. I hope it gives you a sense of closure or clarity of the meaning behind my writing.

It was an early, sunny afternoon on the beach of Cancun, Mexico. The roaring waves called me, inviting me. I couldn't resist the pull; the tides felt magnetic. I was surprised by the vibes between me and the ocean tides because I was tired and had intended to rest on the beach. As I skipped into the water, I began debating if my passion to swim stemmed from a need to escape any sense of confinement, or a need to cope with feeling broken. Then, loud whistles pierced through the air and shook me out of my translucent thoughts. I should have paid attention to the lifeguard's warnings. But the Caribbean Sea had already swept me.

My tendency for gullibility increases on the beach, allowing the calm of the waves to be deceiving more often than not. I felt alarmed as the tides picked me up and swallowed me, further away from shore. Every effort I made to get closer to the shallow end seemed pointless when the tidal waves crashed in on me at a steady pace. My thoughts drifted into the worst possible scenario. *"How will I make it out? I'm exhausted. I need to keep my pace and breathe. I think an appointment with death is here."* Another wave landed on me and I snapped out of my fears. *"NO! Did you forget the swimmer in you? The fighter in you? This is not how you are going to end."* I picked up my feet, my heart powered up, and my mind propelled into full force, borrowing the strength of the ocean tides. It was in me all along, as I used the calm between the waves to sprint forward, diving underwater to take me closer to shore. My mind led the way. I dived under before the rise and kept forward, full force aiming toward the shore.

I couldn't resist the sense of relief to know that there was still a stamina in me that I thought was gone. My spirit-fighting mode finally met ground level. I stayed in a state of shock when a sudden phenomenon of strength awoke in me. The sea had opened its heart to me, to show me that I'll be okay. The ocean taught me that it's okay to be more in tune with myself than I was with others. The high tides took me under and whispered, "It's okay to borrow our energy." That was the moment I trusted the earth's promise to keep me safe in ways no one else could.

I learned more about empowerment than I ever thought possible. It wasn't frightening to apply a renewed spiritual strength to my journey moving forward. It's okay to be empowered once and for all. The moments of panic in the sea were transformed into energy that had been dormant for far too long. My last collision with the ocean tides was a promise sealed to walk me through my unsettled battles. After all, my desire to fly stems from the first time I learned to swim.

When I finally stepped out of the liberating blue waters and stumbled onto shore, my legs felt like rubber elastics. I felt intoxicated by tidal rhythms and I was sure that I looked that way too.

When I faced the lifeguard, he glared at me, but I knew he wouldn't understand what I had to say for myself, so I smiled in peace. My daughter looked comforted to see me as I approached a seat and dropped my body with its weight to carry another story for the rest of my life.

I realized that many panic attacks that I've experienced were not in fear of losing anything and anyone I love; they were in fear of losing myself completely and not being able to keep the things and people I love from being swept away from me. Surviving far from the shallow didn't just awaken my power, it taught me that I can save myself and that's why I can save the ones who accept my love too. Because without a loving fight between the heart and soul, the oceans wouldn't survive the motions of the moon and there wouldn't be a life to live.

I hope I have sparked motivation in you to share your true story of survival. Don't be afraid to shine some light on yourself! Each person has their own journey through life and love. All that you have endured, the pain, the effort and time that you invest to make improvements, adds real purpose and depth to your life. If you could see the beauty of resilience, like sky gazers see the stars brighten winter nights, if you could see the beauty of resilience, like sailors follow a summer morning twilight to guide their journey, you could see your individual resiliency. We don't need to be what anyone else expects us to be if we can see love and strength individually. You can learn to love and catch yourself before losing yourself. If you believe the best of yourself, you will not rely on anyone to tell you what you want to hear. If you need someone to make you feel whole, that same person can break you too. So trust only in yourself to feel complete. You possess your own true story of survival, don't be afraid to go in-depth and rise with it.

ACKNOWLEDGEMENTS

To each angel in my life. I know it must have been painful to live on earth because you were meant only for heaven.

I'm so grateful for all the battles, pain, growth, truth and most of all, the amazing people that I have been able to connect to. Thank you, to all who are true with what they give.

To an amazing mentor, editor and coach Iman Hamid, you blessed me every step of the way while sharing your experience in self-publishing.

I'm truly grateful to Sara Bawany for her wonderful assistance with editing my work. It's the beauty of giving and sharing that counts.

To all the stars that I held the first day they were born: My children, you are the gems of my heart. To my parents who, after all my hardships, understood me more than ever before. And to my brothers and sisters, friends and family who stood by me from day one. My dear friends, fellow poets and authors on Instagram who have inspired and supported me. Thank you with all my heart and soul.

Far From The Shallow

ABOUT THE AUTHOR

Linda Musleh is a Canadian writer and poetess, who values writing as healing therapy. She writes about mental health, love and heartbreak. Linda first started her collection of poetry on Instagram, known as @bella.m.poetry, where she was inspired by fellow poets and readers who could resonate with her work. Linda hopes that her poetry and prose moves her readers and offers them assurance that they are not alone and there is a broader, brighter path through pain and suffering. Linda is a devoted mother and a physical and mental health advocate. Her passion is to help those in need of healing and peace. In her spare time, Linda enjoys swimming, dance and music as motivations for a deeper sense of freedom and positivity.

Far From The Shallow

Thank you so much for reading.
If you enjoyed this collection, please consider leaving a review on Amazon and/or Goodreads.

Manufactured by Amazon.ca
Bolton, ON